INVESTIGATING SCIENCE CHALLENGES

Investigating

HEAT

Richard Spilsbury

CRABTREE
PUBLISHING COMPANY
WWW.CRABTREEBOOKS.COM

CRABTREE
PUBLISHING COMPANY
WWW.CRABTREEBOOKS.COM

Author: Richard Spilsbury

Editors: Sarah Eason, Jennifer Sanderson, Petrice Custance, Reagan Miller

Proofreaders: Kris Hirschmann, Janine Deschenes

Indexer: Wendy Scavuzzo

Editorial director: Kathy Middleton

Design: Emma DeBanks

Cover design and additional artwork: Emma DeBanks

Photo research: Rachel Blount

Production coordinator and prepress technician: Tammy McGarr

Print coordinator: Katherine Berti

Consultant: David Hawksett

Produced for Crabtree Publishing Company by Calcium Creative

Photo Credits:

t=Top, tr=Top Right, tl=Top Left

Inside: Shutterstock: Alphaspirit: p. 20; BkkPixel: p. 21; Corbac40: p. 8; Dar1930: p. 19t; Drohn: pp. 1, 26-27; DW labs Incorporated: p. 6; Foto Cuisinette: p. 4; India Picture: p. 12; Daniel Jedzura: p. 9; Vasin Lee: p. 7; Martin Novak: p. 13; Ivan Smuk: p. 15t; Thanamat Somwan: p. 25r; Manfred Steinbach: pp. 24-25; Dmytro Vietrov: pp. 14-15; Marian Weyo: p. 5; YK: pp. 18-19. Corbac40: p. 8

Cover: Tudor Photography.

Library and Archives Canada Cataloguing in Publication

Spilsbury, Richard, 1963-, author
      Investigating heat / Richard Spilsbury.

(Investigating science challenges)
Includes index.
Issued in print and electronic formats.
ISBN 978-0-7787-4206-7 (hardcover).--
ISBN 978-0-7787-4265-4 (softcover).--
ISBN 978-1-4271-2010-6 (HTML)

      1. Heat--Juvenile literature. 2. Thermodynamics--Juvenile literature. I. Title.

QC256.S655 2018   j536   C2017-907738-4
                                                               C2017-907739-2

Library of Congress Cataloging-in-Publication Data

Names: Spilsbury, Richard, 1963- author.
Title: Investigating heat / Richard Spilsbury.
Description: New York New York : Crabtree Publishing, [2018] | Series: Investigating science challenges | Includes index.
Identifiers: LCCN 2017059668 (print) | LCCN 2017060180 (ebook) | ISBN 9781427120106 (Electronic HTML) | ISBN 9780778742067 (reinforced library binding) | ISBN 9780778742654 (pbk.)
Subjects: LCSH: Heat--Juvenile literature. | Thermodynamics--Juvenile literature.
Classification: LCC QC256 (ebook) | LCC QC256 .S655 2018 (print) | DDC 536--dc23
LC record available at https://lccn.loc.gov/2017059668

Crabtree Publishing Company
www.crabtreebooks.com   1-800-387-7650

Printed in the U.S.A./022018/CG20171220

Published in Canada
Crabtree Publishing
616 Welland Ave.
St. Catharines, Ontario
L2M 5V6

Published in the United States
Crabtree Publishing
PMB 59051
350 Fifth Avenue, 59th Floor
New York, New York 10118

Published in the United Kingdom
Crabtree Publishing
Maritime House
Basin Road North, Hove
BN41 1WR

Published in Australia
Crabtree Publishing
3 Charles Street
Coburg North
VIC, 3058

CONTENTS

WHAT IS HEAT?

Every day, we use heat in many different ways. We use hot water to clean ourselves and our clothes. We use heat to cook our food and keep our homes warm.

This stove gives off heat. The heat can be used to cook and heat food.

Heat Energy

Heat is a form of **energy**. Energy is the power or ability to make things move, work, or happen. Light and sound are forms of energy, too. All forms of energy can be transferred, or moved from one place to another. On a cold day, we might sit close to a heater so we can feel its warmth moving through the air toward us. Heat is the energy stored inside something. When something is hot, it has a lot of heat energy and when it is cold, it has less.

Temperature and Heat Energy

Temperature is a measure of how hot or cold something is. We can measure temperature using a **thermometer**. Thermometers measure temperature in units called degrees Fahrenheit (°F) or degrees Celsius (°C). Heat energy and temperature are not the same thing. A mug of hot chocolate and a bathtub full of water can be the same temperature. However, the water has more heat energy because there is a lot more of it.

Water boils at 212 degrees Fahrenheit (100 degrees Celsius) and freezes at 32 degrees Fahrenheit (0 degrees Celsius).

INVESTIGATE

Scientists **observe** the world around them and ask questions. They then plan and carry out **investigations** to find answers. In this book, you will carry out investigations to answer questions about heat. On pages 28 and 29, you can find investigation tips, check your work, and read suggestions for other investigations you can try.

SOURCES OF HEAT

A heat **source** is something that can release or make heat. There are many different sources of heat. Some occur in nature and are called natural heat sources. Humans create some heat sources for their own use. These are called human-made heat sources.

The Sun

The Sun is a natural heat source. It is the biggest heat source in our **solar system** and is the nearest star to planet Earth. Like other stars, its surface is covered with very hot **gases** that mix together and cause reactions in its core, or center. The reactions create a lot of heat energy. This makes the Sun incredibly hot. Heat energy from the Sun travels through space to warm us on Earth.

The Sun keeps Earth at just the right range of temperatures for living things to survive.

Heat Above and Below Earth

There are other sources of heat in nature, too. **Geothermal energy** is a type of heat energy produced and stored in the form of steam or hot water beneath Earth's surface. This type of energy can be collected, or harnessed, and used to heat homes and buildings. There is also a huge amount of heat energy inside a bolt of lightning, which can strike and start a fire or cause an **electrical outage**.

A bolt of lightning can reach temperatures of 50,000 degrees Fahrenheit (27,760 degrees Celsius), which is 5 times hotter than the surface of the Sun.

Other Sources of Heat

Fuels, such as wood and gasoline, are sources of heat energy. When we burn fuels from plants, such as wood from trees, heat energy is released. This kind of heat energy is originally from the Sun. Plants use energy from the Sun to grow. They store some of this energy to use as food. We also use fuels, such as coal, to make electricity. Electricity powers stoves that provide heat energy we can cook with, and heating systems to keep homes warm in winter.

WARMING UP

Heat energy does not stay in one place. It moves from one object to another. If heat energy is added to something, that thing's temperature becomes higher. The transfer of heat from one object to another, through direct contact, is called **conduction**.

heat from the stove →

The heat from the flame on the stove warms the pot. The pot transfers heat to the water or food contained inside.

How Conduction Works

When we heat vegetables in a frying pan or a pizza on a tray in the oven, we are using conduction to make a hot meal. Heat from the stove flows by conduction into the pan that sits on the stove. It warms up the food inside it. Heat moves through some solids very quickly. When you take a metal spoon from a drawer, it usually feels cold at first. If you hold it for a while, it quickly warms up because your body's heat conducts through it rapidly.

What Materials Are Good Conductors?

Materials that allow heat to flow through them are called **conductors**. Some materials are better conductors of heat than others. Cooking pans are made of metal because metal is an excellent conductor of heat. Metal lets heat move through it easily and quickly. The handles on a pan are usually made from a material such as wood or plastic. These materials are not good heat conductors. This stops them from getting hot, so you can lift the hot metal pan without burning your hands.

Woks are made of thin steel, which is a good conductor of heat. This makes the wok ideal for stir-frying food at hot temperatures.

INVESTIGATE

When you are on a playground or in a park on a hot, sunny day, try touching the different pieces of equipment and other things outside. Touch objects such as metal slides, wooden benches, and plastic swing seats. Which materials feel hot to the touch? Which object feels the coolest? Why do you think this is?

Let's Investigate

CHOOSING SPOONS

Conduction is the transfer of heat energy from one substance to another through direct contact. Do you notice how some materials get hotter faster when they touch something hot? Some materials are better heat conductors than others. Let's investigate heat conduction of different materials.

You Will Need:
- A plastic, metal, and wooden spoon, all of equal size
- A small glass bowl
- A butter knife
- Cool, soft butter
- 3 equal-sized small beads
- Boiling water from a kettle
- A stopwatch
- A sheet of paper
- A pen
- An adult to help

Step 1: Place the plastic spoon in the glass bowl with the handle part downward. The rounded part of the spoon should rest just above the bowl's edge.

Step 2: Use a knife to spread a small amount of butter onto the tip of the spoon. Push a bead into the butter. Ask an adult to fill the glass bowl with boiling water. Be careful! Hot water can burn.

10

Step 3: Start timing with the stopwatch as soon as the hot water is added to the bowl. Every two minutes, use words and pictures to record what is happening to the butter and the position of the bead. Continue for eight minutes. If the bead slides off the spoon, record how long it took to do so.

Science Challenge

Step 4: Repeat the experiment using the metal and wooden spoons. First, choose the spoon you think will melt the butter and drop the bead faster than the plastic spoon. Use what you have learned in this book about heat conduction and different materials. Repeat the steps and record your results. Then repeat the experiment with the third spoon.

Challenge Questions

- Which spoon did you think would melt the butter and drop the bead fastest? Explain your thinking.
- Which of the three spoons was the poorest conductor? Which was the best?
- Why is the bead helpful in this experiment?
- Why is it important to repeat the experiment using the same amount of butter, and beads and spoons of the same size?

COOLING DOWN

Things cool down because heat energy can move from place to place. Heat always moves from a warmer object or location to a cooler object or location. As heat energy moves from the warmer object, it becomes cooler and its temperature decreases. The cooler object receiving the heat energy becomes warmer and its temperature increases. You can see this happening when your ice cream starts to melt when you are out in the sunshine.

When we have an infection, we often get a fever because our bodies are fighting the germs causing it. Fevers raise body temperature, which can make us sicker. Putting a cold cloth or ice pack on the head allows heat to flow from the body so it cools down.

When Do Things Stop Cooling Down?

Have you noticed that when you leave a hot drink on a table and come back to it later, it has become cold? In fact, it will be the same temperature as the room you left it in. Heat spreads out from hotter objects to colder objects until they are the same temperature. Heat stops moving when the temperatures of the two objects are the same.

When we have baked muffins or a cake and they are too hot to eat, we leave them out for a short time to make them cool enough to enjoy.

How Do We Keep Cool?

To keep cool, remember that heat always flows from hot objects toward cold objects. If a room is too warm, we can open a window so some of the warm air flows outside toward the cooler air there. If an oven is too hot, we can leave the door open for a few minutes so that the hot air flows out. When people are too hot, their skin looks red. This happens because blood flows near the surface of the skin, which allows the heat from the blood to flow into the air around the person's body.

INSULATION

There are many times in our lives when we do not want things to cool down or become hotter. **Insulators** are materials that slow down or keep heat from moving from place to place. We put our lunch in an insulated bag to keep it cool. Wearing a coat stops heat from escaping from our warm bodies when we leave a heated house on a cold winter day.

Feathers are good insulators, so people wear feather-filled jackets when they are snowboarding. The feathers trap a lot of air and keep the wearers warm.

How Insulation Works

Insulators are not sources of heat. They cannot produce heat or warm something that is cold. Insulators hold in heat that is already there by keeping it from moving or passing through them. If you wrap your warm body in a wool or fleece blanket, the blanket acts as an insulator. It keeps heat from flowing away from your body into the air.

Air as an Insulator

Air is a good insulator if it is trapped effectively between two solid materials. For example, some oven mitts have thick layers of fabric that trap air between them. They protect the wearer's hands by stopping the heat from hot pans reaching their skin and burning them. A thermos bottle keeps drinks warm or cool by trapping a warm layer of air between outer and inner sections.

In this **thermal image**, the red color shows where heat is being lost from the house. The roof is blue because the attic has insulation materials that stop heat from escaping.

INVESTIGATE

Some materials make better insulators than others, just as some substances make better heat conductors than others. As insulators do the opposite job of conductors, do you think materials that are poor conductors would make good insulators? Wood, plastic, paper, and textiles, such as wool, are poor conductors. Are they good insulators?

15

Let's Investigate

CUP COOLERS

On a hot day, do you notice how a cooler keeps bottles of water cold and refreshing, yet a bottle of water in a backpack warms up? Coolers work because their insulating middle layer slows the conduction of heat from outside to inside. Let's investigate which materials make the best insulators.

You Will Need:

- A small plastic cup
- A large plastic cup into which the small cup will fit
- Cotton balls
- A tablespoon
- A jug of warm water
- Plastic food wrap
- A rubber band
- A freezer
- A stopwatch
- A notepad
- A pencil
- Foam cups, ripped into pieces
- Aluminum foil, ripped into pieces

Step 1: Place the small cup inside the large cup. Pack the gap between the two cups, including the bottom, with flattened cotton balls. You will need to pack the cotton balls tightly to fill the spaces completely so there are not too many air gaps.

Step 2: Add three tablespoons of warm water to the small cup. Cover the top of the large cup with plastic food wrap and secure it with a rubber band. Put it in the freezer.

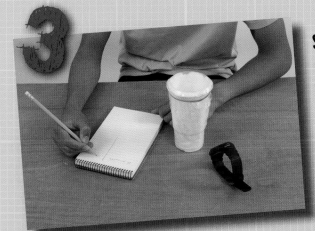

Step 3: Check the cup every 15 minutes to see if ice has formed on the water inside the small cup. Use words and pictures to record any changes in the state of the water. How long does it take for a layer of ice to form?

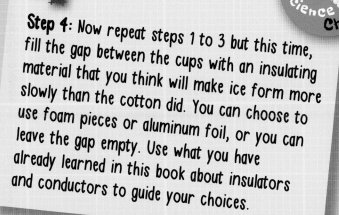

Step 4: Now repeat steps 1 to 3 but this time, fill the gap between the cups with an insulating material that you think will make ice form more slowly than the cotton did. You can choose to use foam pieces or aluminum foil, or you can leave the gap empty. Use what you have already learned in this book about insulators and conductors to guide your choices.

Science Challenge

Challenge Questions

- Which insulator did you choose to use between the cups and why?
- What was the difference in time for an ice layer to form between the cups insulated with the cotton balls and the material you chose?
- Based on the results of your experiment, which of the materials was the worst insulator? Explain your answer.
- Why it is important to use the same amount of water at the same temperature in both tests?

CONVECTION

Conduction carries heat through solids. When **fluids**, such as gases and liquids, are free to move, they can carry heat energy with them. This is called **convection**. Convection is very useful in our everyday lives. It allows us to heat water or soup, and it allows a heater to warm a whole room.

Some birds glide higher into the sky by spreading their wings and catching a lift on hot air that is rising by convection.

Convection in Air

Convection is one of the ways our homes heat up when we turn on the heating system. The air all around us is a type of gas. When we turn on a heater, the air above it warms up and rises. This causes colder air to drop closer to the heater. Soon, the air is moving in what we call a **convection current**, which warms up the entire room. Convection currents also create wind outside. When the land **absorbs**, or soaks up, heat from the Sun, it warms up the air above it. As this warm air rises, cooler air flows in to take its place. This moving air is wind.

Convection in Liquids

When you put a pot of soup on a stove, heat from the stove warms the pot. Then the soup touching the bottom of the pot warms up. Warm liquids and gases are less **dense** and lighter than cold ones, so the warmed area of soup rises. When this happens, the colder soup above the rising warmed soup falls downward. The soup starts to move in a convection current. The current causes heat to spread throughout the pot, until the entire pot of soup is boiling.

Convection currents in a pot of liquid circulate the heat energy until all the contents are hot.

ABSORBING AND REFLECTING HEAT

Conduction and convection rely on heat energy passing from one object or substance to another. If you sit near a fire, you will feel the heat even though you are not in contact with the fire. The heat you can feel travels by **radiation**.

Solar thermal panels absorb heat from the Sun to warm water for heating homes and also for washing.

Radiation

Radiation, also called **infrared** radiation, is energy that is carried from a hot object by invisible rays. Infrared rays move in straight lines, at the **speed of light**, and do not need air to travel. That is why the Sun can warm our planet from millions of miles away in airless space. Hotter objects emit, or give off, more radiation than cooler objects. Radiation is very useful for carrying out many tasks, such as toasting bread in a toaster. The toaster's wires radiate heat to toast the surfaces of the bread.

Surface Effects

All objects absorb and emit some radiated heat energy, but the amount depends on what their surfaces are like. Dark-colored and **matte** surfaces, such as paved roads or rooftops, absorb more radiation than light-colored or shiny surfaces, such as those used on spacecraft, which **reflect** infrared radiation.

Shiny suits help keep firefighters from becoming too hot by reflecting away heat energy radiated by fires.

INVESTIGATE

You can feel heat absorption at work when you walk on a sidewalk or road wearing thin shoes and your feet feel hot. The materials used to make sidewalks and roads store heat energy. They emit infrared radiation long after the hottest part of the day has passed, even into the night. What other surfaces would you expect to cool down slowly, based on the appearance of their surfaces and their ability to absorb a lot of radiation and release their heat slowly?

ON THE SURFACE

Have you ever noticed that you feel warmer when you wear a black T-shirt on a sunny day than you do when you wear a white one? This is because of the way radiation is absorbed or reflected. Let's investigate how different materials absorb radiation.

You Will Need:

- A pair of scissors
- 2 sheets of black paper
- 3 identical clear plastic cups
- 6 rubber bands
- 2 sheets of white paper
- 2 sheets of aluminum foil
- 3 ice cubes
- A stopwatch
- A notepad
- A pencil
- A sunny day

THINK!

Step 1: Cut the black paper to the same height as the cups. Wrap it around one cup to cover the entire outside surface. Hold it in place with rubber bands, one at the top and one at the bottom.

Step 2: In the same way, cover another cup in white paper and the last cup in aluminum foil.

Step 3: Put one ice cube into each cup. Then, put the cups outside in the sunshine. To make the test accurate, you must use ice cubes that are the same size and ensure each one is exposed to the same amount of sunlight. Put a piece of black paper on top of the cup covered in black paper, a piece of white paper on top of the cup covered in white paper, and a piece of foil on top of the foil-covered cup.

Science Challenge

Step 4: Use the information you have learned about how radiation is absorbed or reflected to predict which cup the ice cube will melt in first. Which of the three materials do you think will keep the ice cube solid for the longest amount of time? Check the state of the ice in each cup every five minutes. Record your findings.

Challenge Questions

- Which cup's ice cube melted first? What does this tell you about the material?
- What was the time difference between when the first and the last ice cubes melted?
- Was there a difference in reflection between the cups covered in white paper and foil? If there was a difference, explain why you think this was the case.
- Why is it important to use ice cubes that are the same size and ensure each one is exposed to the same amount of sunlight?

CHANGING ENERGY

Heat energy, like every other kind of energy, can change from one form to another. Energy cannot be created or destroyed. For example, most light energy that we use to light up our world comes from hot objects that burn brightly. These include anything from a lit candle or bonfire to the Sun. When released, some of the heat energy changes into light energy. Light from heat energy is called **incandescence**.

When the **kinetic energy**, or movement energy, of tires spinning is restricted by **friction**, some energy transforms into heat. This makes the tires heat up.

Heat from Fuel

People can use energy changes in many useful ways. To get heat energy from wood, people burn it. Burning changes the **chemical energy** stored inside the wood into heat (and light) energy, and even some sound energy too as the fire crackles. Power plants make electricity by changing the chemical energy in fuel, such as coal or oil, into heat. The heat is used to turn a **turbine** that works the **generator** that releases electrical energy. Electrical energy can be changed back into heat for use on stoves and in heaters.

Candles provide a soft, simple form of light resulting from the energy transformation of incandescence.

Movement and Heat

Have you ever wondered why people rub their hands together quickly to warm them up when it is cold? The movement causes friction, which is the force that resists motion between two surfaces. The friction changes the kinetic energy (movement energy) into heat energy to make our hands feel warmer. If people rub dry sticks together quickly, the friction converts the kinetic energy into enough heat for the sticks to catch fire.

INVESTIGATE MORE

Heat is a vital form of energy. Many living things rely on heat produced inside their bodies or taken from their surroundings to survive. The Sun, fires, and volcanoes are all natural heat sources. Electric heaters and radiators are human-made heat sources. All heat energy comes from other forms of energy. For example, chemical energy in fuel transforms into heat energy when burned.

Moving Heat

Heat moves from hotter to colder objects in different ways. Conduction is when heat energy gets passed on from one solid to another. Convection is when heat energy moves through liquids or gases. Radiation is when invisible infrared rays carry heat energy from warm objects. Heat energy can either be absorbed or reflected by the different surfaces it radiates toward. Dark-colored, matte surfaces absorb heat much better than light-colored, shiny surfaces.

Trapping Heat

The atmosphere is a blanket of gases surrounding Earth. The gases trap some of the Sun's heat, keeping Earth warm enough for living things to survive. By burning **fossil fuels** such as coal, oil, and natural gas, people have increased the amount of certain gases in the atmosphere. These extra gases trap more heat on Earth, increasing the average global temperature. This is known as global warming. Global warming is believed to be responsible for the melting of the polar ice caps and increasing numbers of extreme weather events such as hurricanes.

Heat energy is one of the most important forms of energy for the survival of many living things.

INVESTIGATE

You could investigate the different ways we use heat energy. For example, how do refrigerators use heat energy to cool down food? What are ground source heat pumps and how do they work? How do mirrors help use the Sun's heat to make electricity in a solar thermal power plant? What other amazing uses of heat energy can you learn about?

Science Challenge
TIPS

Pages 10-11: Choosing Spoons

You should notice that the butter on the metal spoon melts quickest and the bead drops fastest. The process is slower on the wooden spoon and slowest on the plastic spoon. Metal conducts heat better than wood, which conducts heat better than plastic. Plastic is the poorest conductor. The bead adds weight to the butter so it slides faster and its speed of melting is easier to see. Using the same amount of butter and same-sized beads ensures that there is a similar volume of material for heat to conduct through. This makes the experiment accurate.

Pages 16-17: Cup Coolers

Foam is the best insulator. If you used foam, you should have noticed that it insulated the cup more effectively than the cotton balls. After foam, cotton is the next-best insulating material. The worst insulator is aluminum foil. Foil is a good conductor of heat. Heat energy moves quickly from the water to the outside of the foil, so it cools and forms ice much faster. Using the same amount of water at the same temperature ensures the experiment is accurate and fair.

To investigate further, you could test other materials to see if they are insulators or conductors. Wrap identical ice cubes in different materials and secure them with rubber bands. Then time how quickly the ice melts.

Pages 22-23: On the Surface

You should see that the ice cube in the cup wrapped in black paper melts first, then the ice cube in the white cup, and finally the foil-covered cup. This is because dark colors absorb more infrared radiation than light colors, and reflective surfaces absorb less than matte surfaces. So the black paper increases in temperature faster than the white paper, melting the ice inside fastest. The foil reflects most radiation, keeping the cube solid for a longer period of time. It is important to use ice cubes that are the same size and to ensure that each one is exposed to the same amount of sunlight to make the investigation fair and accurate.

To take this further, research what colors people wear or use to paint buildings in countries where the average temperatures are hot or cold. Find out how they use color to keep themselves warm or cool.

GLOSSARY

Some bold-faced words are defined where they appear in the text.

absorbs Soaks up

chemical energy A type of energy stored in chemicals, such as sugar and gasoline

conduction The way heat energy is transferred between objects that are touching

conductors Materials or objects that transfer heat energy (and often also electrical energy) well

convection The way heat energy is carried through a fluid such as a gas or a liquid

convection current The way fluid moves or flows when heated by convection

dense A measure of the weight per unit volume of a substance. For example, we say water is denser than oil.

electrical outage Loss of power supply to an area

energy Ability or power to do work

fluids Types of matter, such as a gas or liquid, in which particles of a substance can flow past one another. Fluids take the shape of the container they flow into.

fossil fuels Fuels such as oil, coal, or natural gas that took millions of years to form under the ground from dead plants and animals

friction The action of one object or surface moving across another. Friction is a force that can slow things down.

fuels Materials such as coal, gasoline, or oil that are burned to produce heat or power

gases Substances that are often invisible, do not keep their shape, and expand to fill any amount of space

generator A machine that makes electricity

geothermal energy Energy released from heat found deep within Earth

infrared Rays of light at the red end of the light spectrum that are invisible to the human eye

insulators Materials that slow the transfer or flow of heat

investigations Procedures carried out to observe, study, or test something to learn more about it

kinetic Relating to or resulting from movement

matte Not shiny

observe To use your senses to gather information

radiation Energy that travels in the form of invisible rays or waves

reflect Bounce or throw back

solar system The collection of planets and moons that orbit or circle the Sun

source A place, person, or thing from which something originates or can be obtained

speed of light The speed at which light travels, up to 186,400 miles (300,000 km) per second

temperature A measure of how hot or cold something is

thermal image An image that shows the heat that is being given off an object

thermometer A device that measures how hot or cold something is

turbine A machine with blades that are turned, such as by the push of steam, water, or wind, usually to operate a generator

LEARNING MORE

Find out more about heat and its uses.

Books

Canavan, Thomas. *Cool Experiments with Heat and Cold* (Mind-Blowing Science Experiments). Gareth Stevens, 2017.

Gardner, Robert, and Eric Kemer. *Experiments With Temperature and Heat* (Science Whiz Experiments). Enslow Publishing, 2017.

Royston, Angela. *The Science of Heat* (Flowchart Smart). Gareth Stevens, 2016.

Sullivan, Laura. *What Is Heat?* (Unseen Science). Cavendish Square Publishing, 2016.

Websites

Find out some fun facts about heat at:
www.ducksters.com/science/heat.php

Learn more about heat energy at:
www.explainthatstuff.com/heat.html

This site features a game to help you learn more about conductors and insulators:
www.sciencekids.co.nz/gamesactivities/keepingwarm.html

INDEX

About the AUTHOR

Richard Spilsbury has a science degree, and has had a lifelong fascination with science. He has written and co-written many books for young people on a wide variety of topics, from ants to avalanches.